EASY PIANO

PITCH PERFECT & PITCH PERFECT 2:
Motion Picture Soundtrack Selections

ISBN 978-1-4950-3512-8

HAL•LEONARD®
CORPORATION

7777 W. BLUEMOUND RD. P.O. BOX 13819 MILWAUKEE, WI 53213

Visit Hal Leonard Online at
www.halleonard.com

BACK TO BASICS

Fast Swing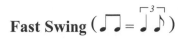

BOOGIE WOOGIE BUGLE BOY

Words and Music by DON RAYE and HUGHIE PRINCE

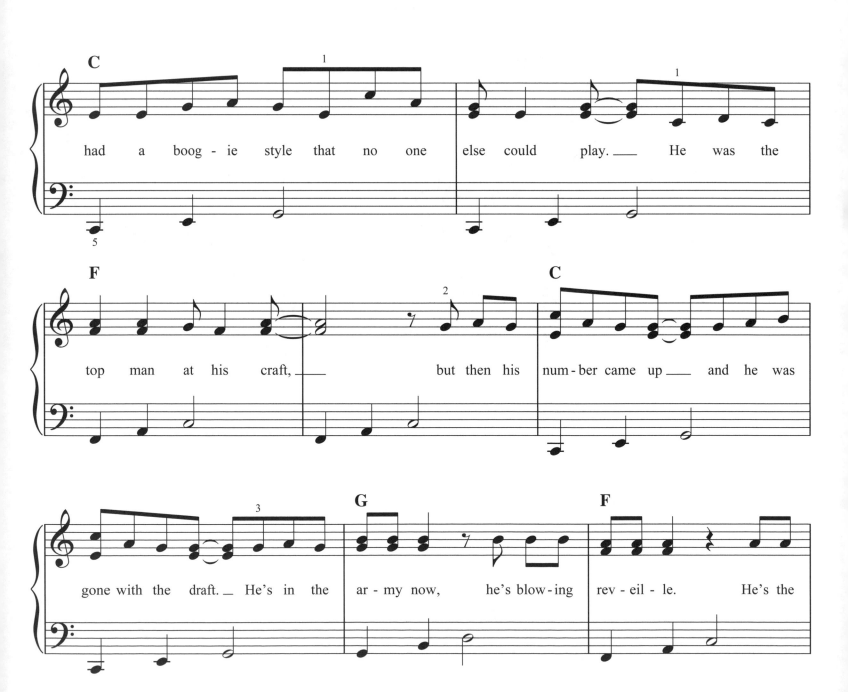

He was a fa-mous trum-pet man from out Chi-ca-go way.___ He

had a boog-ie style that no one else could play.___ He was the

top man at his craft,___ but then his num-ber came up ___ and he was

gone with the draft.__ He's in the ar-my now, he's blow-ing rev-eil-le. He's the

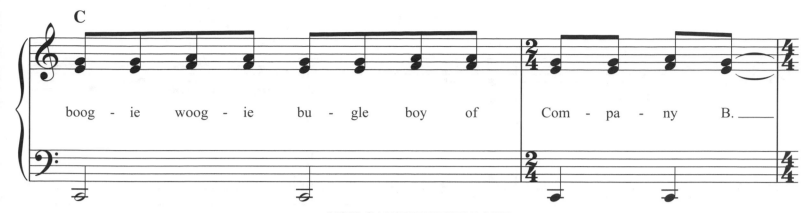

C

boog - ie woog - ie bu - gle boy of Com - pa - ny B.___

YOU CAN'T HURRY LOVE

Words and Music by EDWARD HOLLAND JR.,
LAMONT DOZIER and BRIAN HOLLAND

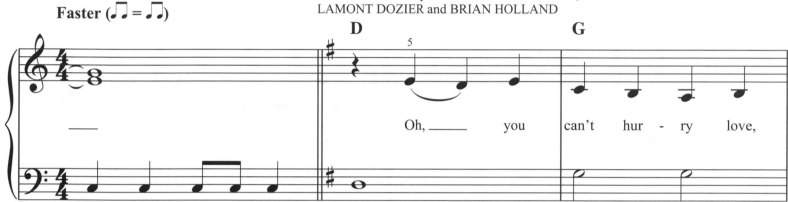

Faster

D   **G**

Oh,___ you can't hur - ry love,

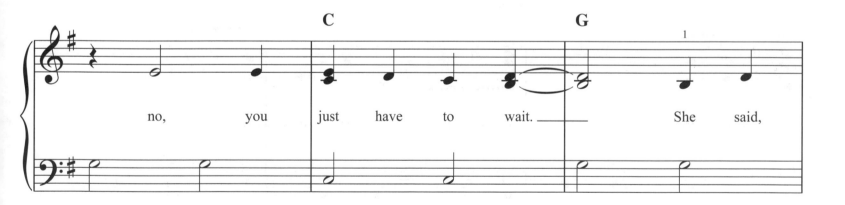

C   **G**

no, you just have to wait.___ She said,

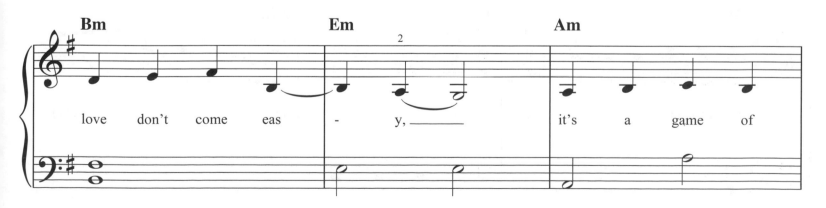

Bm   **Em**   **Am**

love don't come eas - y,___ it's a game of

LADY MARMALADE
*Words and Music by KENNY NOLAN
and ROBERT CREW*

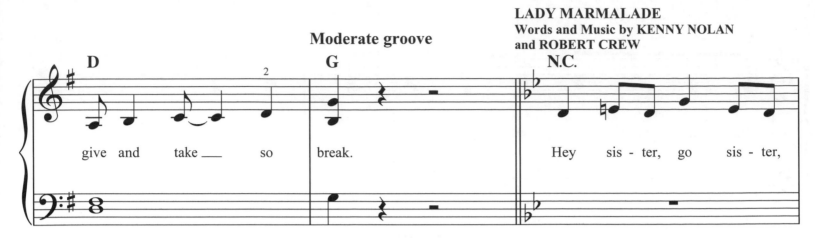

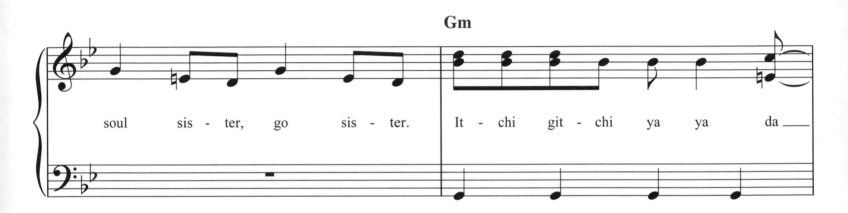

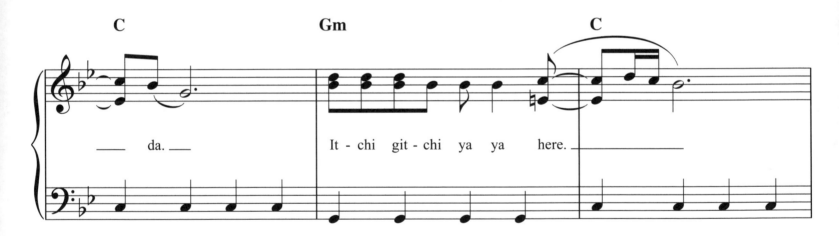

MMMBOP

Words and Music by ISAAC HANSON,
TAYLOR HANSON and ZAC HANSON

8

Laid back (♪♪ = ♪♪)

MY LOVIN' (YOU'RE NEVER GONNA GET)
Words and Music by THOMAS McELROY and DENZIL FOSTER

Nev-er gon-na get it, nev-er gon-na get it, nev - er gon-na get it, nev-er gon-na get it.

Nev-er gon-na get it, nev-er gon-na get it, nev - er gon-na get it. Whoa. ___

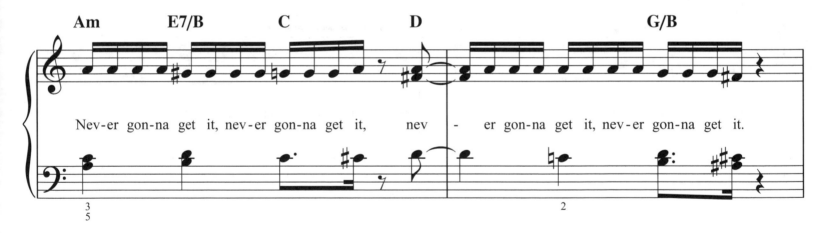

Nev-er gon-na get it, nev-er gon-na get it, nev - er gon-na get it, nev-er gon-na get it.

Nev-er gon-na get it, nev-er gon-na get it, nev - er gon-na get it, nev-er get it.

CUPS
(When I'm Gone)

Words and Music by A.P. CARTER, LUISA GERSTEIN
and HELOISE TUNSTALL-BEHRENS

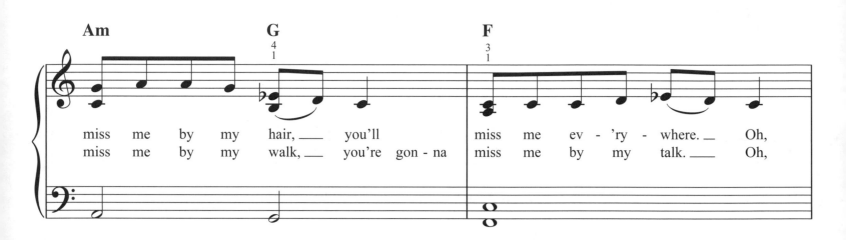

you're gon - na miss ___ me when I'm gone. You're gon - na
you're gon - na miss ___ me when I'm gone. You're gon - na

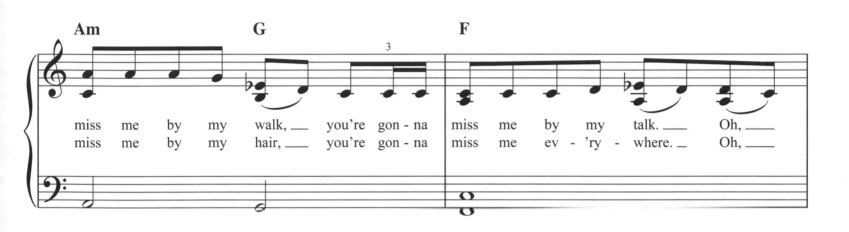

miss me by my walk, ___ you're gon - na miss me by my talk. ___ Oh, ___
miss me by my hair, ___ you're gon - na miss me ev - 'ry - where. ___ Oh, ___

To Coda ⊕

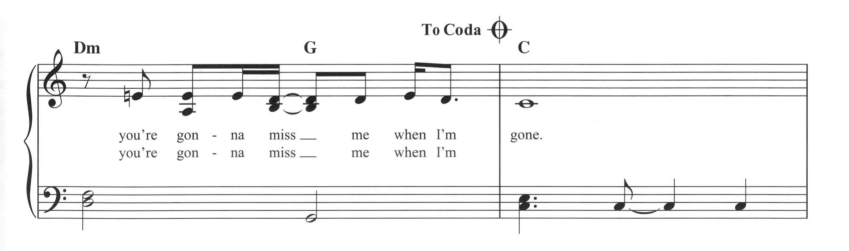

you're gon - na miss ___ me when I'm gone.
you're gon - na miss ___ me when I'm

I got my tick - et for the long way __ 'round,

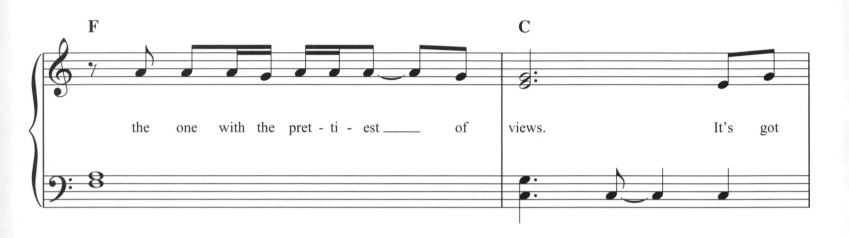

the one with the pret - ti - est ____ of views. It's got

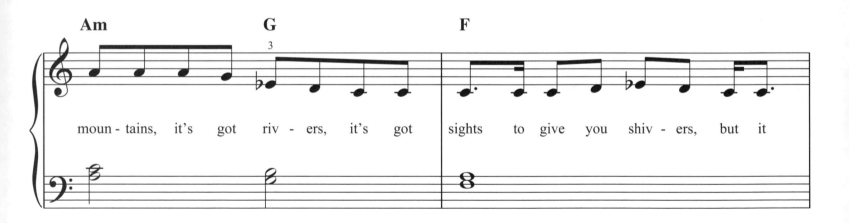

moun - tains, it's got riv - ers, it's got sights to give you shiv - ers, but it

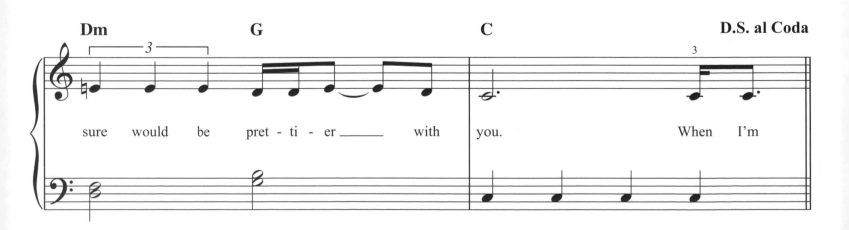

sure would be pret - ti - er ____ with you. When I'm

CODA

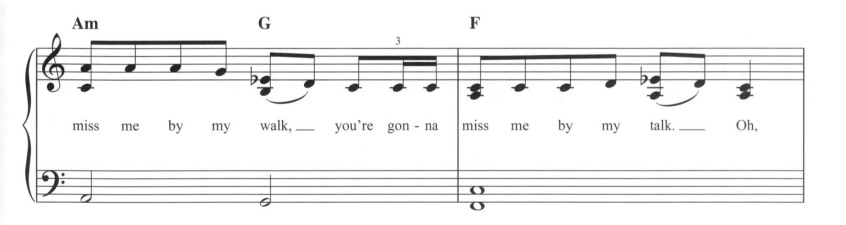

FLASHLIGHT

Words and Music by SIA FURLER,
CHRISTIAN GUZMAN, SAM SMITH,
JASON MOORE and MARIO MEJIA

Moderate Ballad

When to-mor-row comes, _ I'll be on my own,

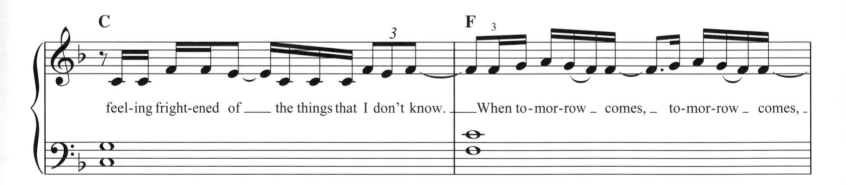

feel-ing fright-ened of _ the things that I don't know. _ When to-mor-row _ comes, _ to-mor-row _ comes, _

_ to - mor - row _ comes.

And though the road is long, _ I look up to the sky.
I see the shad - ows long be-neath the moun-tain-top.

And in the dark I found _ lost hope that I won't fly,
I'm not a-fraid _ when the rain won't stop,

and I sing a-lone, I sing a-lone,
'cause you light the way, you light the way,

then I sing a-lone. _____
you light the way. _____

I got all I need when I got you and I. ____

I look a-round me and see sweet life.

I'm stuck in the dark, but you're my flash-light.

You're get-ting me, get-ting me through the night. ____

Can't stop my heart when you're shin-ing in my

CUPS
(When I'm Gone)

Words and Music by A.P. CARTER, LUISA GERSTEIN
and HELOISE TUNSTALL-BEHRENS

Moderate Folk

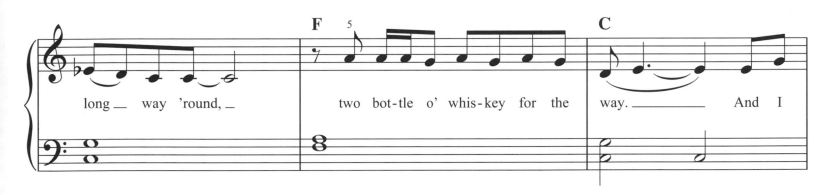

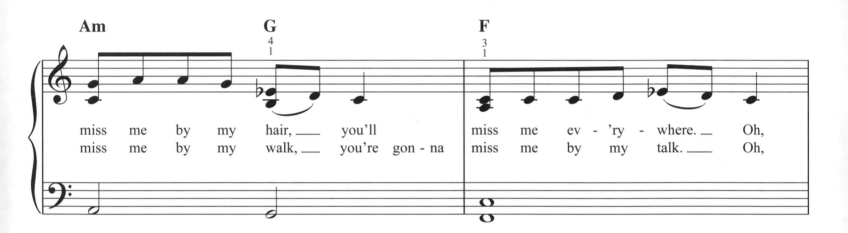

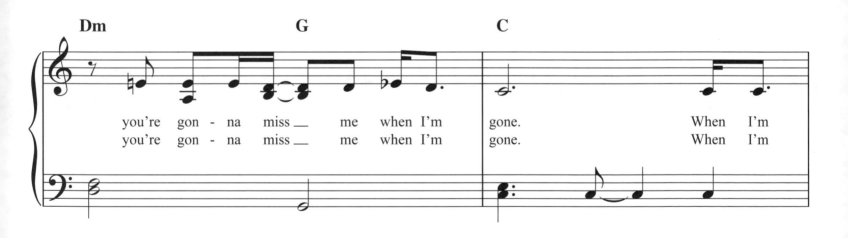

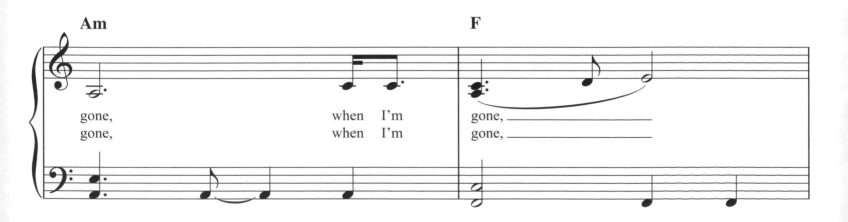

I got my tick-et for the long way __ 'round,

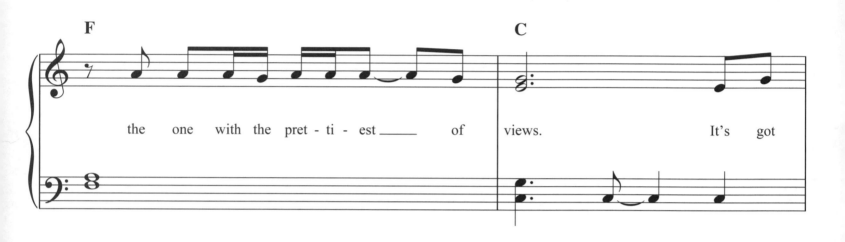

F ... **C**

the one with the pret-ti-est ___ of views. It's got

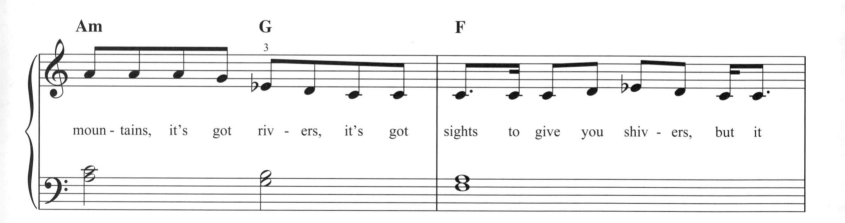

Am ... **G** ... **F**

moun-tains, it's got riv-ers, it's got sights to give you shiv-ers, but it

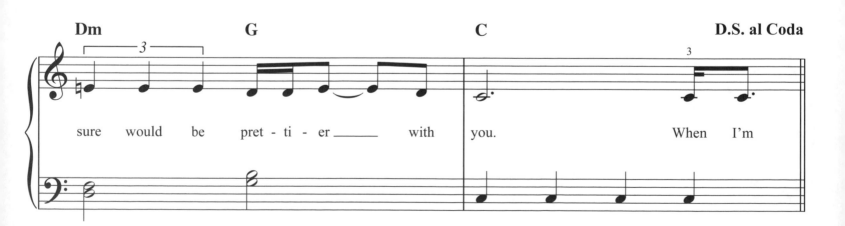

Dm ... **G** ... **C** ... **D.S. al Coda**

sure would be pret-ti-er ___ with you. When I'm

CODA

gone.   When I'm   gone,   when I'm

gone, _____   you're gon-na miss __ me when I'm   gone.   You're gon-na

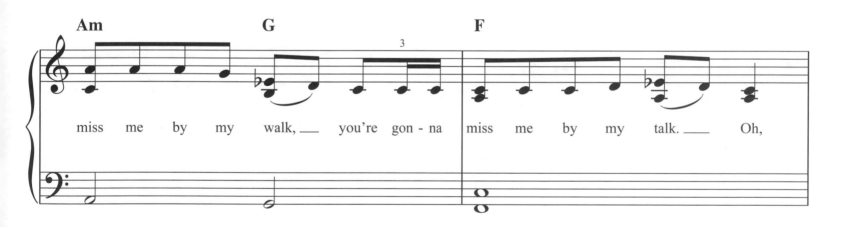

miss me by my walk, __ you're gon-na   miss me by my talk. __   Oh,

you're gon-na miss __ me when I'm   gone.

FLASHLIGHT

Words and Music by SIA FURLER,
CHRISTIAN GUZMAN, SAM SMITH,
JASON MOORE and MARIO MEJIA

Moderate Ballad

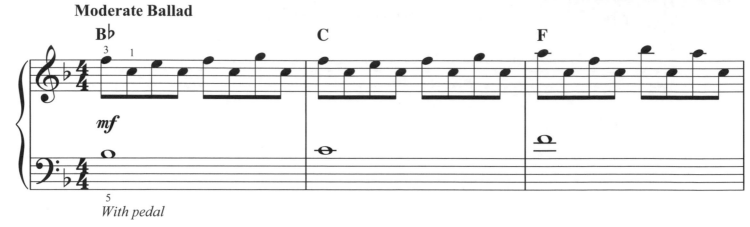

With pedal

When to-mor-row comes, _ I'll be on my own,

feel-ing fright-ened of ___ the things that I don't know. ___ When to-mor-row _ comes, _ to-mor-row _ comes, _

___ to-mor-row _ comes.

And though the road is long, _ I look up to the sky.
I see the shad - ows long be-neath the moun-tain-top.

And in the dark I found _ lost hope that I won't fly,
I'm not a - fraid _ when the rain won't stop,
and I sing a - lone, I sing a - lone,
'cause you light the way, you light the way,

then I sing a - lone. _
you light the way. _

I got all I need when I got you and I. _

I look a-round me and see sweet life.

I'm stuck in the dark, but you're my flash-light.

You're get-ting me, get-ting me through the night. _

Can't stop my heart when you're shin-ing in my

eyes; can't lie, it's a sweet _____ life. I'm stuck _ in the dark, but you're my flash‑light.

You're get‑ting me, get‑ting me through the night. _____ 'Cause you're my flash -

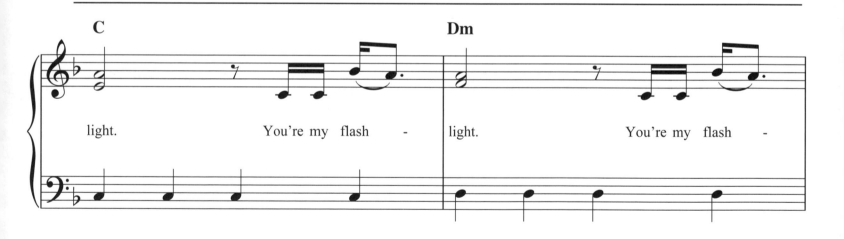

light. You're my flash - light. You're my flash -

light. _____ Oh. _____ You're get‑ting me, get‑ting me through the night. _

Don't you feel the pas - sion? Read - y to ex - plode.

D.S. al Coda

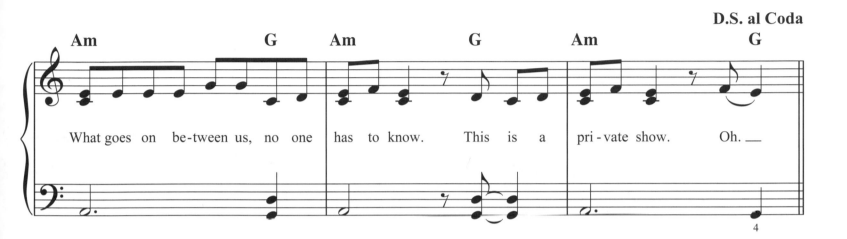

What goes on be-tween us, no one has to know. This is a pri-vate show. Oh. ___

CODA

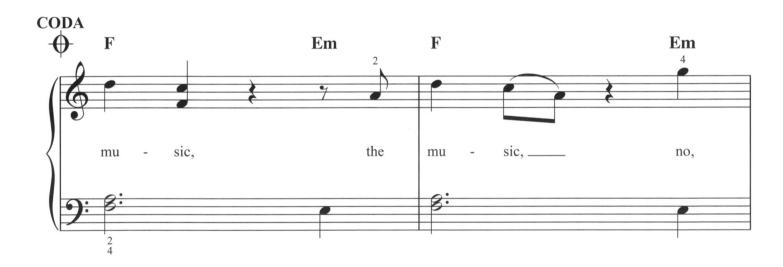

mu - sic, the mu - sic, ___ no,

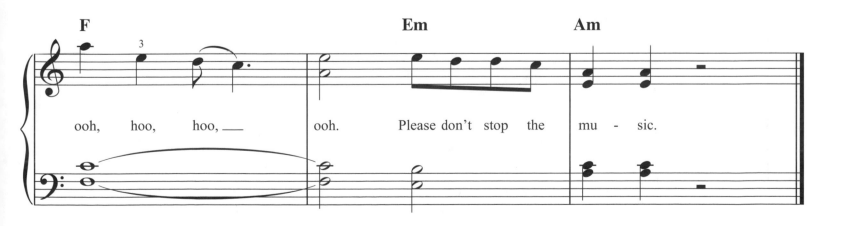

ooh, hoo, hoo, ___ ooh. Please don't stop the mu - sic.

JUMP

Words and Music by ALPHONSO MIZELL, BERRY GORDY JR.,
DEKE RICHARDS, FREDDIE PERREN, JERMAINE DUPRI,
CLARENCE SATCHELL, GREGORY WEBSTER, LEROY BONNER,
MARSHALL JONES, MARVIN PIERCE, NORMAN NAPIER,
RALPH MIDDLEBROOKS and WALTER MORRISON

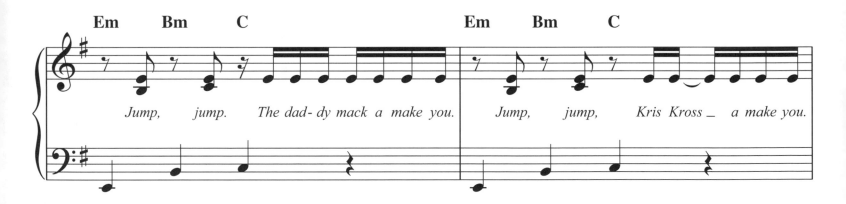

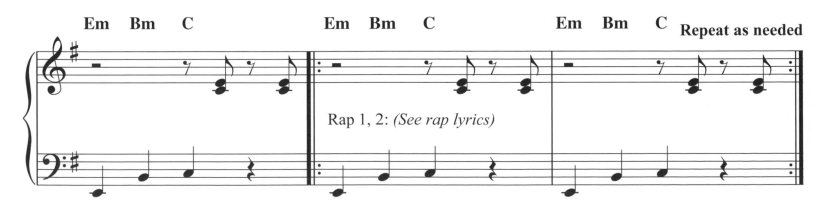

Rap Lyrics

Rap 1: Don't try to compare us 2 another bad little fad
I'm the mack and I'm bad
Givin' you something you never had
I make you bump, bump, wiggle and
Shake your rump
'Cause I be kickin' da flavor that makes
You wanna "Jump"

How high, real high
'Cause I'm just so fly
A young lovable, huggable
Type o' guy
Everything is to the back
With a little slack
'Cause inside out is
Wigada, wigada, wigada, "Wack"

I come stumpin' with something pumpin'
To keep you jumpin'
R&B rappin' bull crap
Is what I'm dumpin'
Ain't nothing soft about Kris Kross
We all dat
So when they ask do they rock
Say believe dat
Chorus

Rap 2: I like my stuff knockin' "Knockin'"
I love it when da girlies
Be like jockin', "Jockin'"
The D.A. double D.Y.M.A.C.
Yeah you know me
I got you jumpin' and bumpin' and pumpin'
Movin' all around "Gee"
I make the six step back
They try to step to the mack
Then they got jacked
To the back you be sportin' your gear
Is that coincidental
"Act like you know and
Don't be claiming that it's mental"

Two li'l kids with a flow
You ain't never heard
Ain't nuttin' faking
You can understand every word
As you listen
To the smooth, smooth melody
The daddy makes you J.U.M.P.
Chorus

LOLLIPOP

Words and Music by
MIKA

Bright tempo

Suck-in' too hard on a

lol-li-pop,— oh, love's gon-na get you down.—

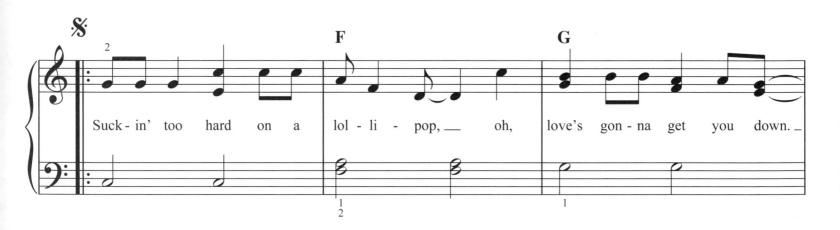

Suck-in' too hard on a lol-li-pop,— oh, love's gon-na get you down._

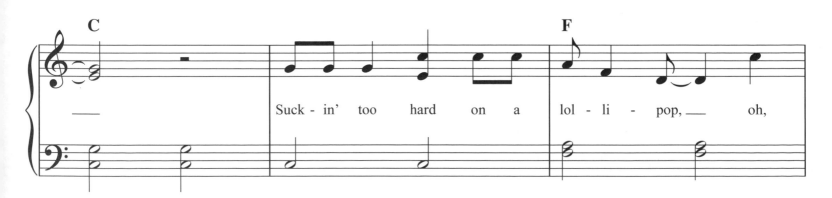

Suck-in' too hard on a lol-li-pop,— oh,

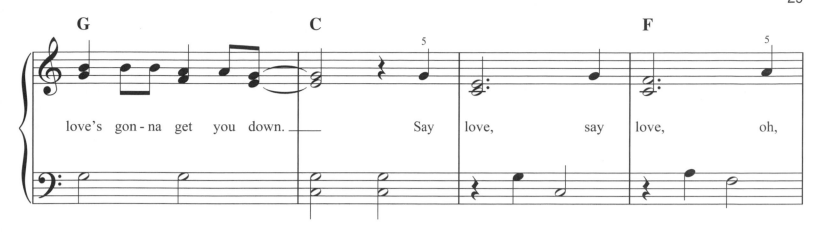

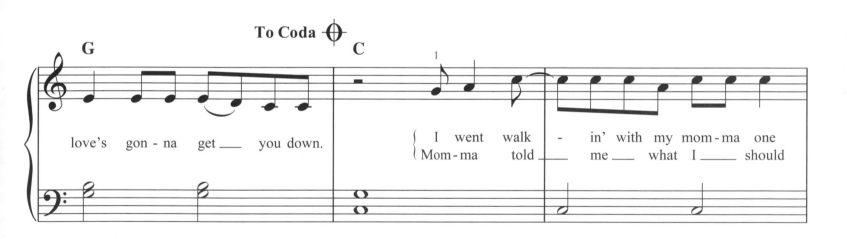

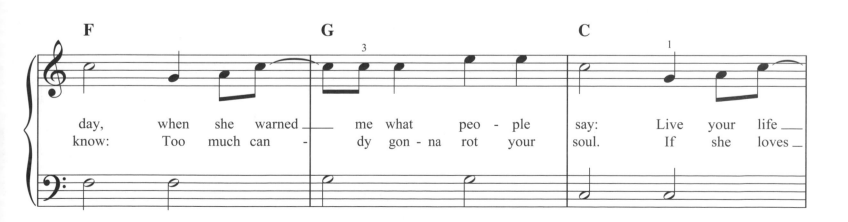

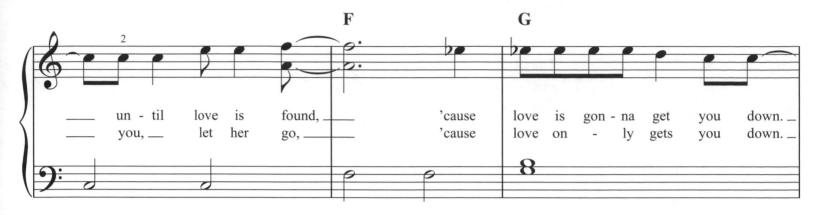

un - til love is found, _____ 'cause love is gon - na get you down. _____
you, _____ let her go, _____ 'cause love on - ly gets you down. _____

Take a look _____ at the girl next door; she's a play -
Take a look _____ at a boy like me; nev - er stood _____

- er and a down - right boor. Je - sus loves _____ her; she wants
_____ on _____ my own two feet. Now I'm blue _____ as I can

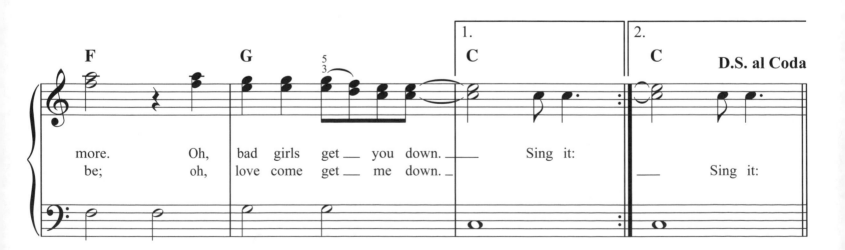

more. Oh, bad girls get _____ you down. _____ Sing it:
be; oh, love come get _____ me down. _____ Sing it:

1. C

2. C **D.S. al Coda**

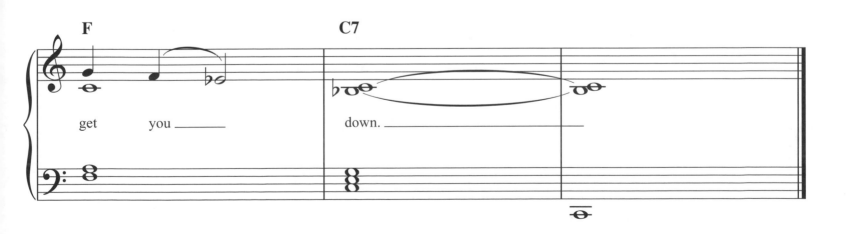

POOL MASHUP
(Just The Way You Are / Just A Dream)

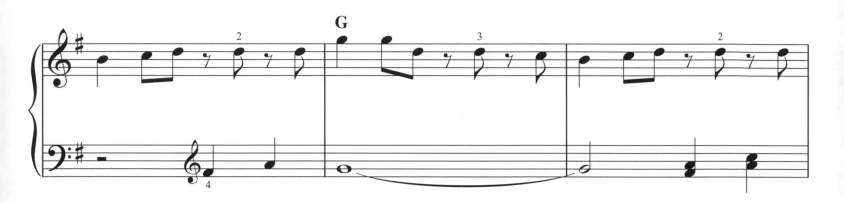

JUST THE WAY YOU ARE
Words and Music by BRUNO MARS,
ARI LEVINE, PHILIP LAWRENCE,
KHARI CAIN and KHALIL WALTON

Oh,   her eyes, __ her eyes __ make the stars look like they're not shin - in'.

JUST A DREAM
Words and Music by CORNELL HAYNES, JR.,
DAMON REINAGLE, DAVID HARRIS,
JAMES SCHEFFER, RICHARD BUTLER
and FRANK ROMANO

C

But ev-'ry time she asks me, "Do I look o - kay?")

It was on - ly just a dream.__

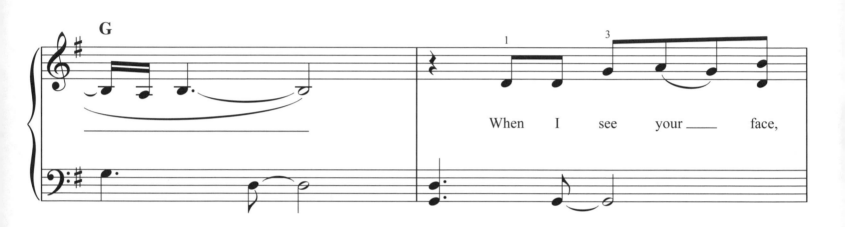

G

When I see your ____ face,

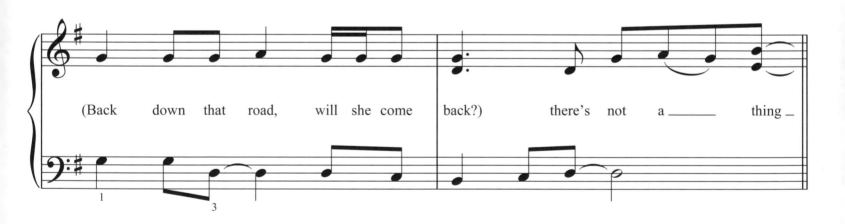

(Back down that road, will she come back?) there's not a ____ thing __

Em7

____ that I ____ would ____ change, ____ 'cause you're a - maz-

WE BELONG

Words and Music by DANIEL ANTHONY NAVARRO
and DAVID ERIC LOWEN

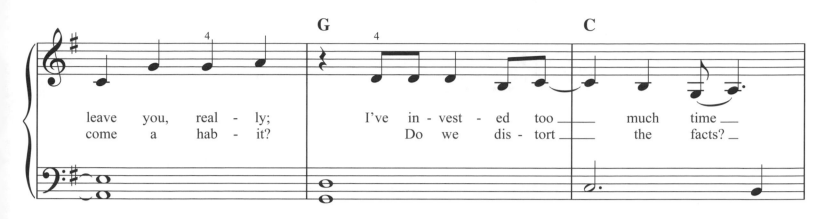

leave you, real - ly; I've in - vest - ed too ___ much time ___
come a hab - it? Do we dis - tort ___ the facts? ___

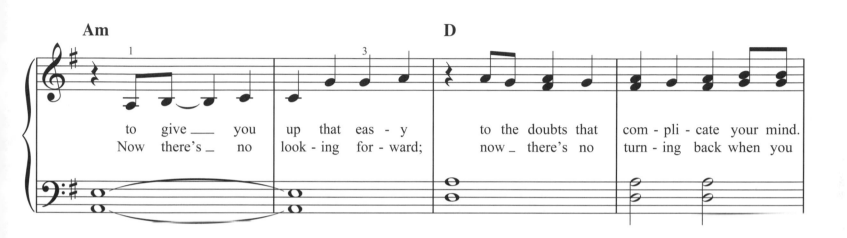

to give ___ you up that eas - y to the doubts that com - pli - cate your mind.
Now there's ___ no look - ing for - ward; now ___ there's no turn - ing back when you

say: We be - long to the light; we be - long to the thun - der.

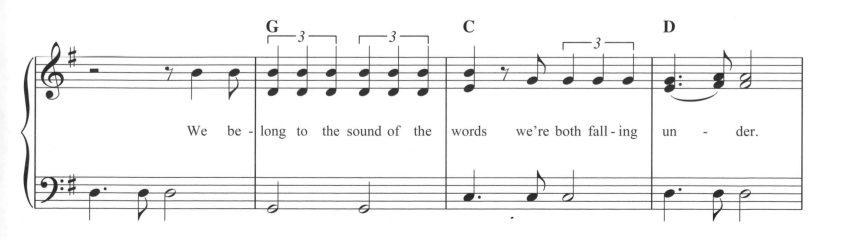

We be - long to the sound of the words we're both fall - ing un - der.

What- ev - er we de - ny or em - brace, for worse or for

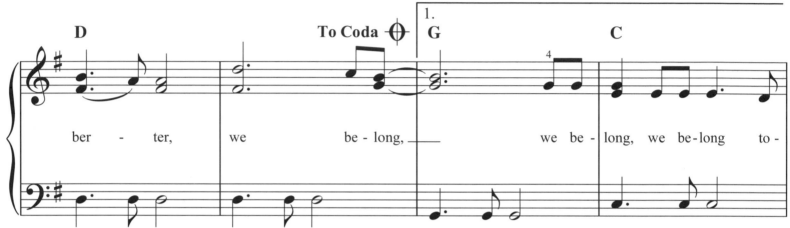

To Coda ⊕ **1.**

ber - ter, we be - long, ___ we be - long, we be-long to-

2.

geth - er. ___ But we're al - ways gon-na be ___ to-

geth - er. Close your...

Close your... Close your eyes and try to sleep, _ now;

close your eyes and try to dream. _ Clear your mind and do your best _ to

try and wash the pal-ette clean. _ You can't _ be - gin to know it,

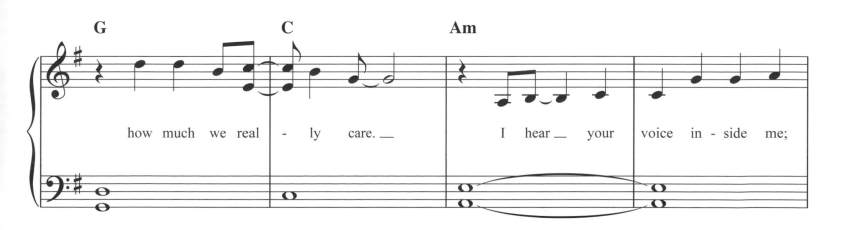

how much we real - ly care. _ I hear _ your voice in - side me;

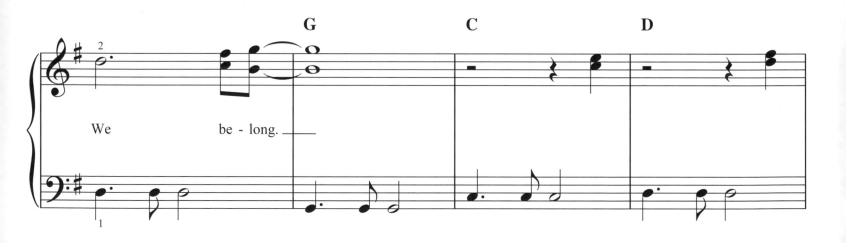

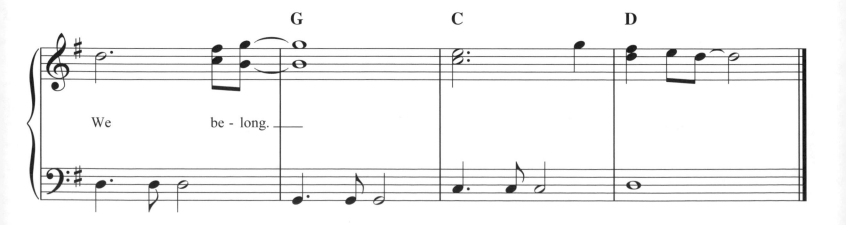

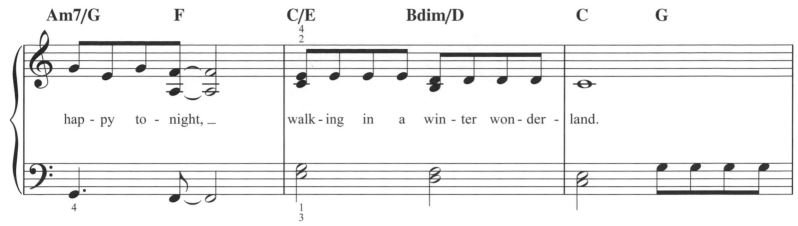

happy to-night, ___ walk-ing in a win-ter won-der - land.

HERE COMES SANTA CLAUS (RIGHT DOWN SANTA CLAUS LANE)
Words and Music by GENE AUTRY
and OAKLEY HALDEMAN

Here comes San - ta Claus, here comes San - ta Claus, right down San - ta Claus

lane. Vix - en and Blit - zen and all his rein - deer

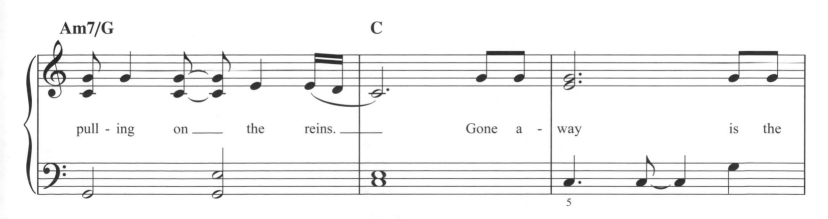

pull - ing on ___ the reins. ___ Gone a - way is the

blue - bird; here to stay is the new bird. He

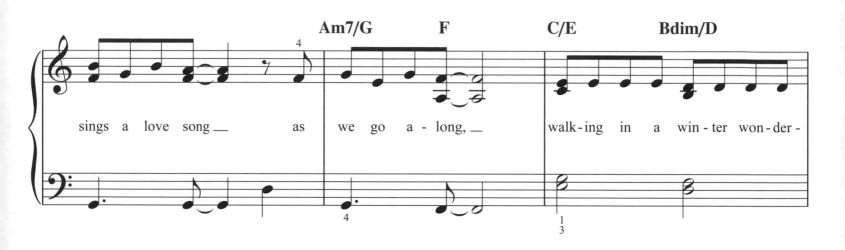

sings a love song ___ as we go a - long, ___ walk-ing in a win-ter won-der-

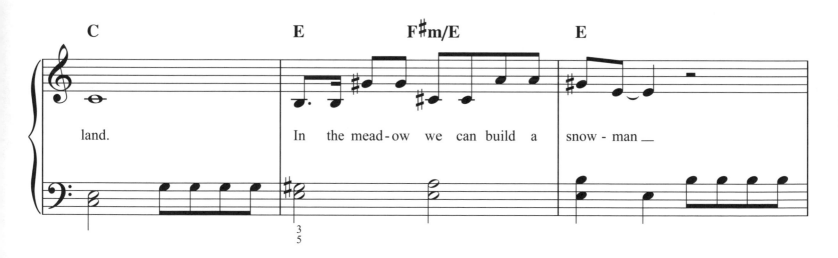

land. In the mead-ow we can build a snow - man ___

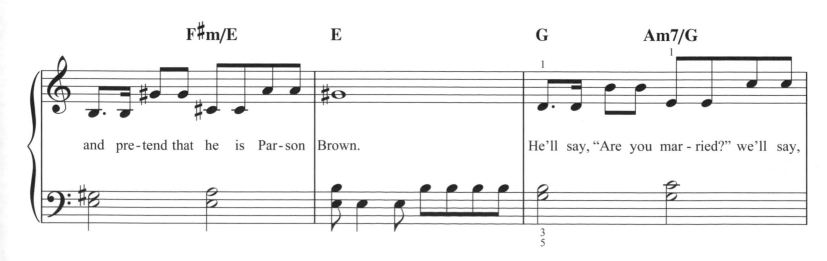

and pre-tend that he is Par-son Brown. He'll say, "Are you mar-ried?" we'll say,

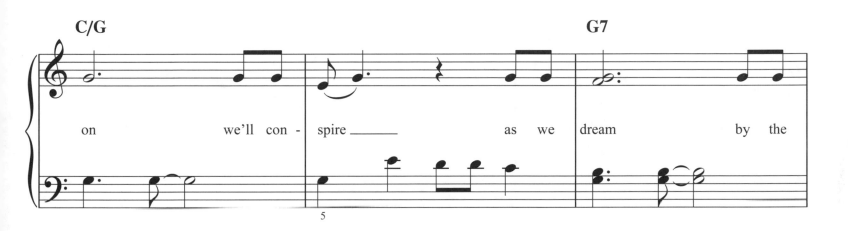

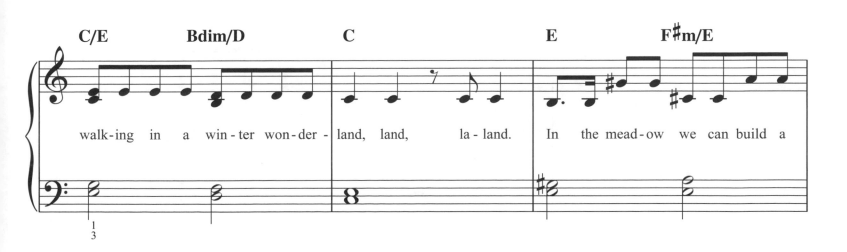

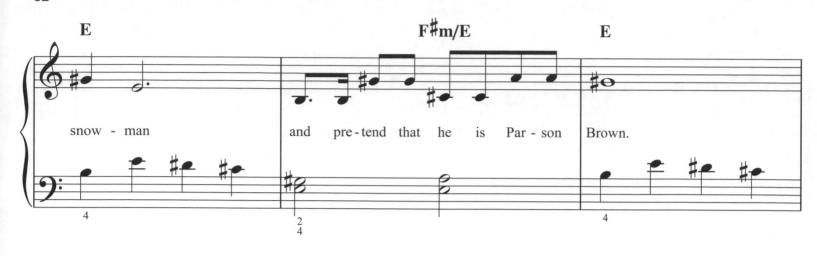

snow - man   and pre-tend that he is Par-son Brown.

We'll have lots of fun with Mis-ter Snow-man, un - til the oth-er kid-dies knock him

down. When it snows, ain't it thrill-ing, though your

nose gets a chill-ing. We'll frol-ic and play ___ the

54

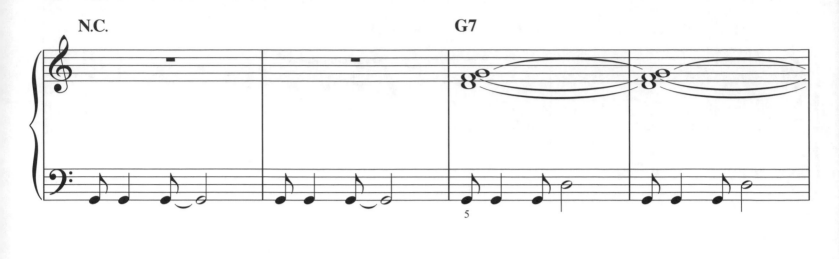

Gone a-

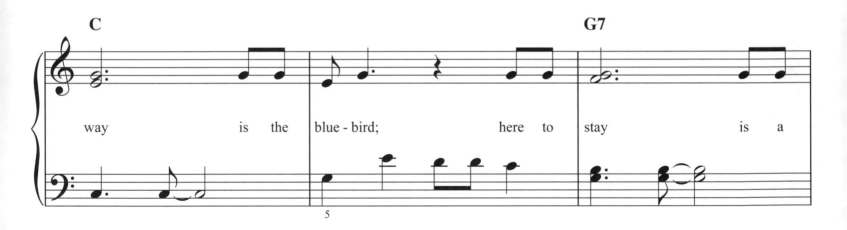

way   is the blue-bird;   here to stay   is a

new bird.   He sings a love song ___   as we go a-long, ___

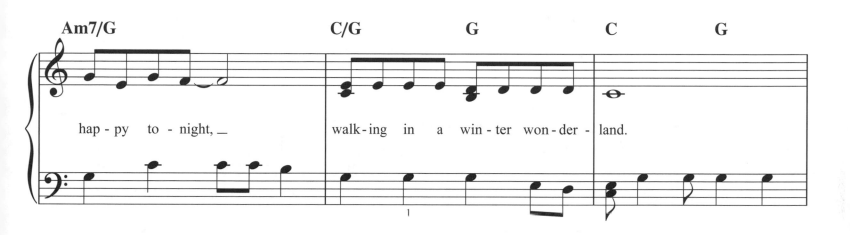

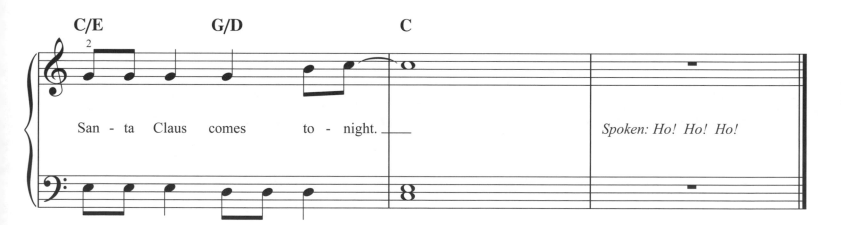

Additional Lyrics

Rap: Once upon a time in the L.B.C.,
Santa came up missing; he was sitting by a tree.
His reindeers was near, but their leader wouldn't lead
So I took the lead. Now, as we proceed...

This ain't for no mistletoe, but you need to listen, yo.
Just in case you didn't know, I call this my Christmas flow.
I could take you higher and higher. Chestnuts roast on an open fire.
"Gone away." Think that's what the, what the song says.

WORLD CHAMPIONSHIP FINALE 2

Moderately

RUN THE WORLD (GIRLS)
Words and Music by BEYONCE KNOWLES,
DAVE TAYLOR, THOMAS PENTZ,
NICK VAN DE WALL, ADIDJA PALMER
and TERIUS NASH

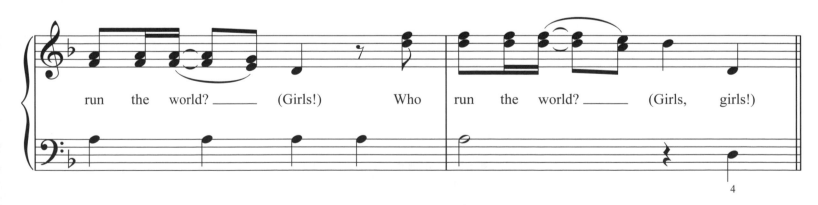

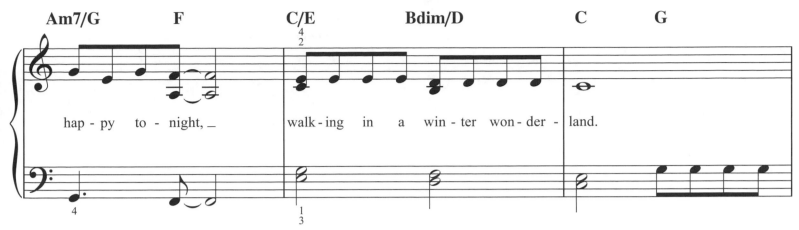

hap - py to - night, __ walk - ing in a win - ter won - der - land.

HERE COMES SANTA CLAUS (RIGHT DOWN SANTA CLAUS LANE)

Words and Music by GENE AUTRY
and OAKLEY HALDEMAN

Here comes San - ta Claus, here comes San - ta Claus, right down San - ta Claus

lane. Vix - en and Blit - zen and all his rein - deer

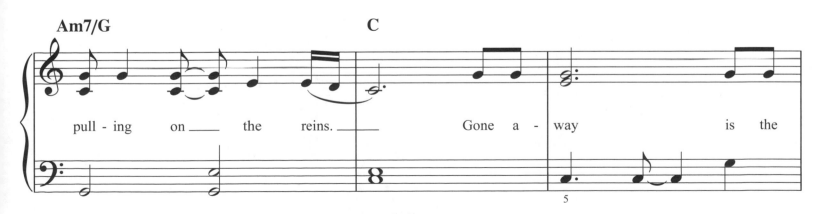

pull - ing on __ the reins. __ Gone a - way is the

blue - bird;　　here to　stay　　　　is the　new bird.　　　He

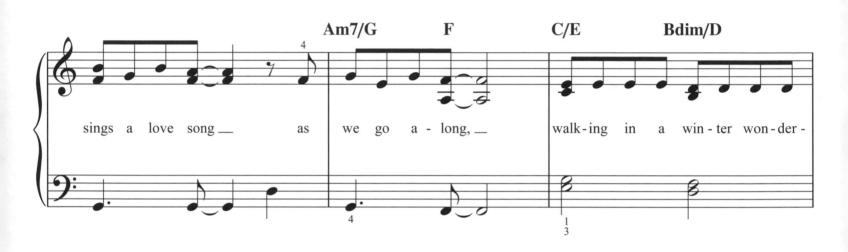

sings a love song ___　　　as　we go a - long, ___　　　walk-ing in a win-ter won-der-

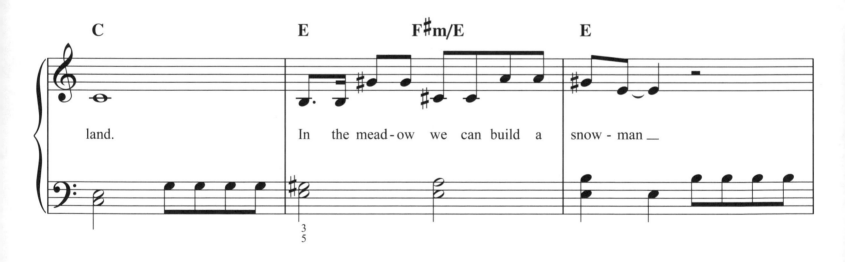

land.　　　In the mead-ow we can build a　snow-man ___

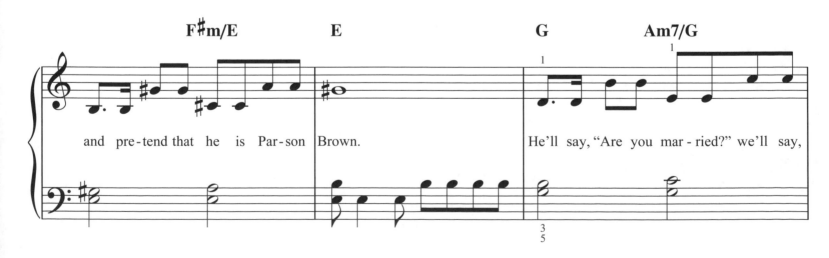

and pre-tend that he is Par-son　Brown.　　　He'll say, "Are you mar-ried?" we'll say,

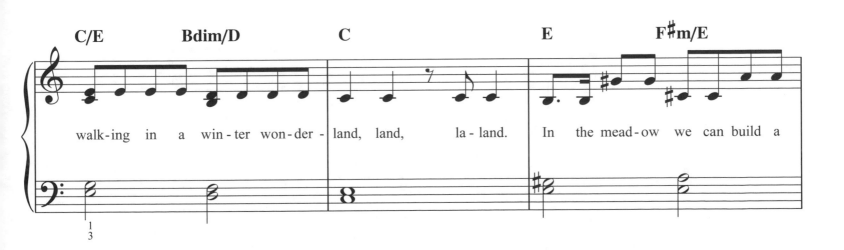

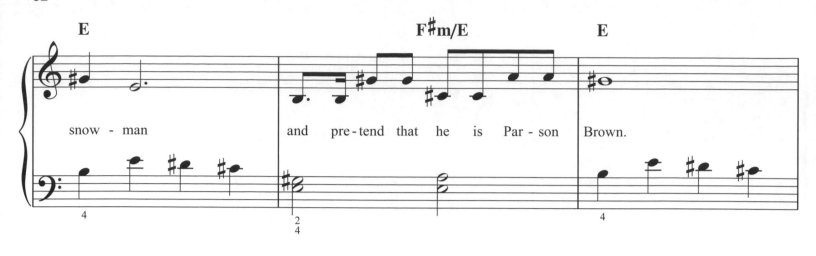

snow-man   and pre-tend that he is Par-son Brown.

We'll have lots of fun with Mis-ter   Snow-man,   un-til the oth-er kid-dies knock him

down.   When it   snows,   ain't it thrill-ing,   though your

nose   gets a chill-ing.   We'll frol-ic and play ___ the

Es - ki - mo way, walk - ing in a win - ter won - der - land. When it

land.

Rap: (See additional lyrics)

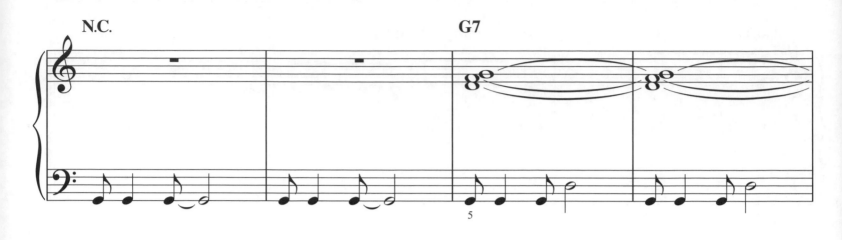

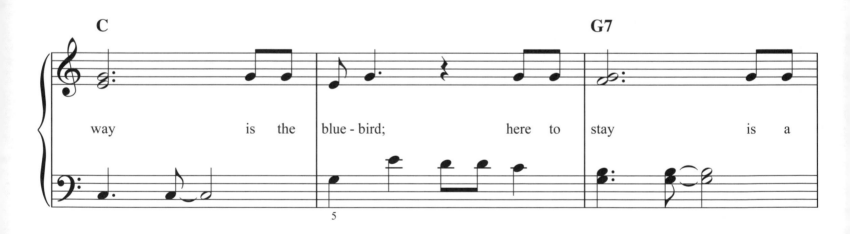

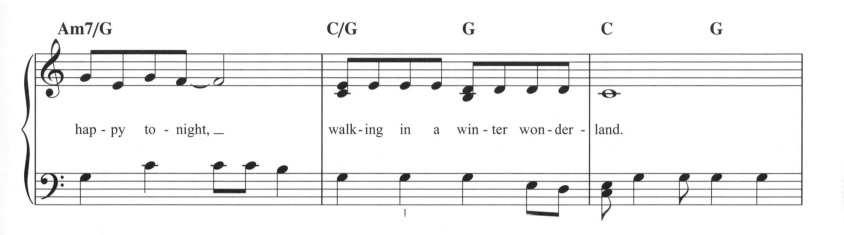

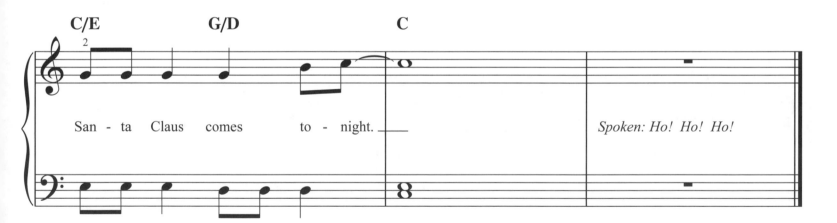

Additional Lyrics

Rap: Once upon a time in the L.B.C.,
Santa came up missing; he was sitting by a tree.
His reindeers was near, but their leader wouldn't lead
So I took the lead. Now, as we proceed...

This ain't for no mistletoe, but you need to listen, yo.
Just in case you didn't know, I call this my Christmas flow.
I could take you higher and higher. Chestnuts roast on an open fire.
"Gone away." Think that's what the, what the song says.

WORLD CHAMPIONSHIP FINALE 2

Moderately

RUN THE WORLD (GIRLS)
Words and Music by BEYONCE KNOWLES,
DAVE TAYLOR, THOMAS PENTZ,
NICK VAN DE WALL, ADIDJA PALMER
and TERIUS NASH

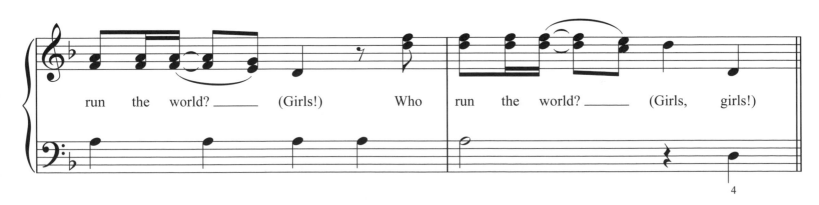

WHERE THEM GIRLS AT

Words and Music by TRAMAR DILLARD, OSCAR SALINAS,
JUAN SALINAS, GIORGIO TUINFORT, JARED COTTER,
ONIKA MARAJ, DAVID GUETTA, SANDY WILHELM
and MICHAEL CAREN

LADY MARMALADE
Words and Music by KENNY NOLAN and ROBERT CREW

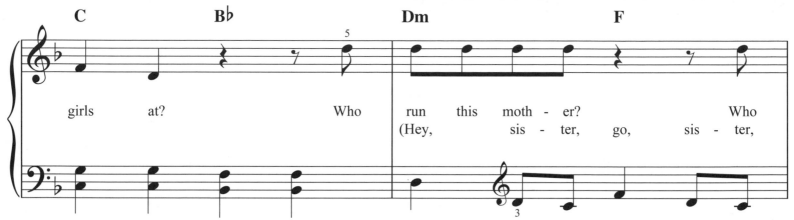

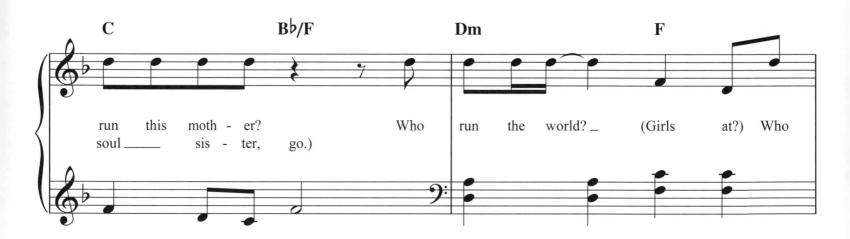

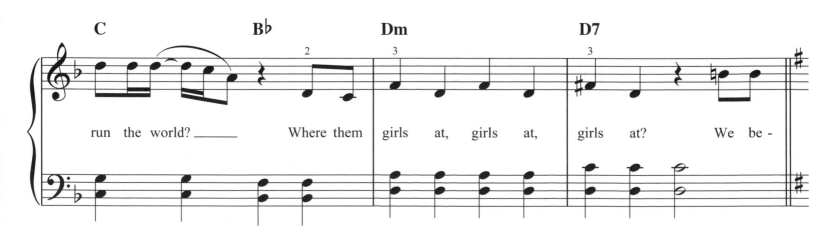

WE BELONG
Words and Music by DANIEL ANTHONY NAVARRO
and DAVID ERIC LOWEN

TIMBER
Words and Music by ARMANDO CHRISTIAN PEREZ, PEBE SEBERT,
KESHA SEBERT, LUKASZ GOTTWALD, HENRY WALTER, BREYAN STANLEY ISAAC,
PRISCILLA RENEA, JAMIE SANDERSON, LEE OSKAR, KERI OSKAR and GREG ERRICO

We run the world. _____ We be - long. ___

Slow groove

FLASHLIGHT

Words and Music by SIA FURLER,
CHRISTIAN GUZMAN, SAM SMITH,
JASON MOORE and MARIO MEJIA

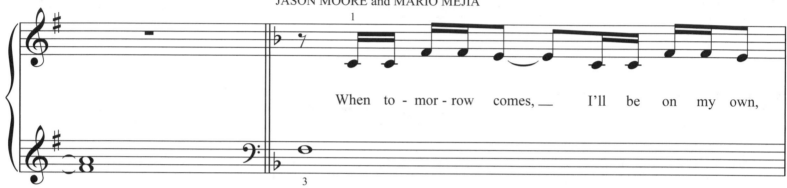

When to - mor - row comes, ___ I'll be on my own,

feel - ing fright - ened of _____ the things that I don't know. When to - mor - row comes, _ when to - mor - row comes,

when to - mor - row comes, _ when to - mor - row comes. And though the road is long, _ I look up to the sky.

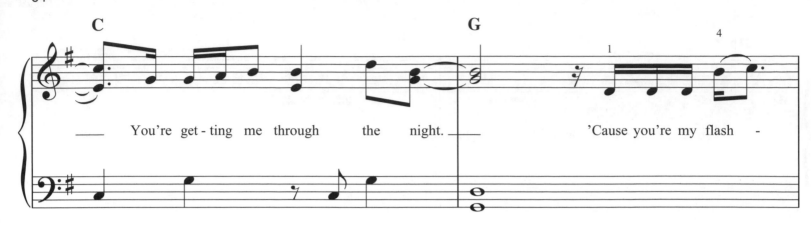

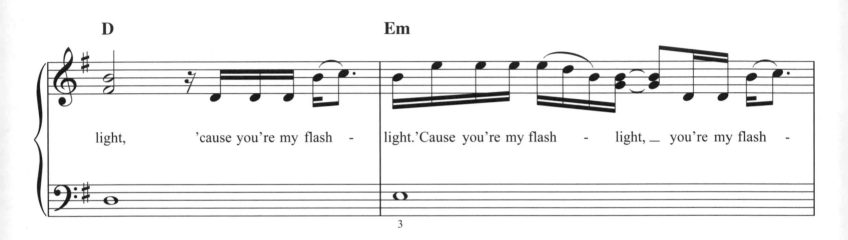